THE EVERYTHING® KIDS' Math Puzzles for Pre-K

Learn about Numbers, Shapes, Patterns, and More with 100 Fun Puzzles!

Hannah Whately

ADAMS MEDIA

NEW YORK LONDON TORONTO SYDNEY NEW DELHI

Adams Media
An Imprint of Simon & Schuster, Inc.
100 Technology Center Drive
Stoughton, Massachusetts 02072

An Everything® Series Book.
Everything® and everything.com® are registered trademarks of Simon & Schuster, Inc.

First Adams Media trade paperback edition July 2021

ADAMS MEDIA and colophon are trademarks of Simon & Schuster.

For information about special discounts for bulk purchases, please contact Simon & Schuster Special Sales at 1-866-506-1949 or business@simonandschuster.com.

The Simon & Schuster Speakers Bureau can bring authors to your live event. For more information or to book an event contact the Simon & Schuster Speakers Bureau at 1-866-248-3049 or visit our website at www.simonspeakers.com.

Interior design by Erin Alexander
Illustrations by Jim Steck

Manufactured in the United States of America

Printed by LSC Communications, Crawfordsville, IN, U.S.A.

1 2021

ISBN 978-1-5072-1612-5

Contents

Introduction

Before ever stepping into a classroom, most children are naturally interested in math. As soon as children learn about the existence of numbers, they want to count—whether it's the number of people in their family or how many crackers they can hold in one hand. You're probably already experiencing a preschooler's enthusiasm and curiosity about the world of numbers. Kids this age love to ask questions and play games as they learn about math. And that's where *The Everything® Kids' Math Puzzles for Pre-K* comes in.

This collection of colorful and fun puzzles and activities is perfect for developing early math skills. The puzzles provide an enjoyable way to learn some important basic math skills before starting kindergarten. Your child will practice counting and comparing numbers, as well as some very basic addition and subtraction. Later puzzles introduce the concepts of sizes and measurements, shapes and patterns, position words, and matching and sorting.

All your child needs are a pencil and some crayons, markers, or colored pencils. And you, of course, to read instructions out loud and encourage your child as they complete the puzzle. Your child will give answers in lots of different ways—by coloring, circling, or putting a checkmark next to an object; tracing a number or shape; and, in some instances, writing a number.

Each chapter features a particular set of math skills. While the puzzles can be done in any order, it's a good idea to move through the ones in the first three chapters from beginning to end, because they increase a bit in difficulty. Mix in puzzles from the last four chapters for variety. Here are the things your child will be learning as you work together on the puzzles and activities:

- **Numbers and counting.** Your child will practice counting, identifying, naming, and ordering numbers up to 10. Objects to be counted are arranged in lots of different ways—for example, in rows or boxes. Encourage your child to count slowly and to touch or point to each object on the page as they count out loud. Some puzzles focus on ordering numbers to 10, both forward and backward, using fun activities like connect the dots, number mazes, and missing number activities. Other puzzles ask your child to find a number and trace it, which gives them practice at forming the numbers. Toward the end of the first chapter, there are puzzles that ask for a number to be written in a box. It may be helpful to have written numbers for them to refer to and copy. If your child is not yet ready for writing numbers, you can always come back to these puzzles at a later time.

- **Comparing numbers.** Your child will explore numbers up to 10 *in relation to each other*. They will decide whether a number is bigger than, smaller than, or the same as another number. They will also look at groups of objects and decide which have more, less, or the same number of items in them.

- **Basic addition and subtraction.** For this early stage, puzzles show only addition and subtraction within 5. They reinforce the idea of addition as joining numbers together and subtraction as taking away. When doing these puzzles, encourage your child to use the pictures to help them. Having counters or blocks on hand may also be helpful for this chapter.

- **Measurement and sizes.** These puzzles help your child become familiar with measurable attributes like height and weight. They will compare objects and say, for example, which is bigger, smaller, or longer. Some puzzles involve matching or sorting according to size.

- **Shapes and patterns.** Your child will become familiar with common two-dimensional shapes, such as circles, squares, triangles, and rectangles. Puzzles in this chapter give your child practice at identifying and naming shapes, spotting them in different situations, and tracing them. Later puzzles will also get your child thinking about the properties of different shapes. Patterning is an important early math skill, and this chapter features puzzles with patterns made from objects, colors, and shapes.

- **Position words, including *inside, outside, between, up,* and *down*.** Preschool children are learning new vocabulary all the time, and these puzzles help them understand words that describe position in a fun and visual way.

- **Matching and sorting skills, and the concepts of *same* and *different*.** Your child will have practice matching and sorting lots of different things, from camels to vegetables!

Don't expect to do too many puzzles in one sitting—a handful of puzzles at a time is best at this age. Likewise, if a puzzle is too hard, don't worry. You can come back to it later. The most important thing is that you and your child have fun working through the book—counting ladybug spots and rubber ducks, measuring wiggly worms, following a shape maze, or sorting laundry. I do hope your child has fun with these puzzles (and learns a bit of math along the way too!).

Chapter 1

Numbers and Counting Up to 10

Preschoolers are just beginning to learn the names for numbers, to count, and to understand what numbers represent. This first group of puzzles will give your child practice at identifying, naming, and ordering numbers up to 10. The activities include lots of counting practice, which you can incorporate into your everyday routine. Encourage your child to count slowly, and point to or touch each object as they count out loud. When the puzzles are done, continue the learning by helping them count objects around them—buttons on a shirt, grapes on a plate, or the members of your family. As you move through the chapter, the puzzles progress in terms of difficulty. Early puzzles introduce individual numbers. Later in the chapter, they focus on ordering numbers, as well as counting to 10, both forward and backward. Some puzzles may require your child to circle, color, or draw a line to their answer, while others may ask them to trace or write a number. All the puzzles reinforce important early number concepts in fun and engaging ways.

Spaghetti and Meatballs

We need lots of tomatoes to make spaghetti sauce!
Find all the tomatoes that show **0** and color them red ➡️

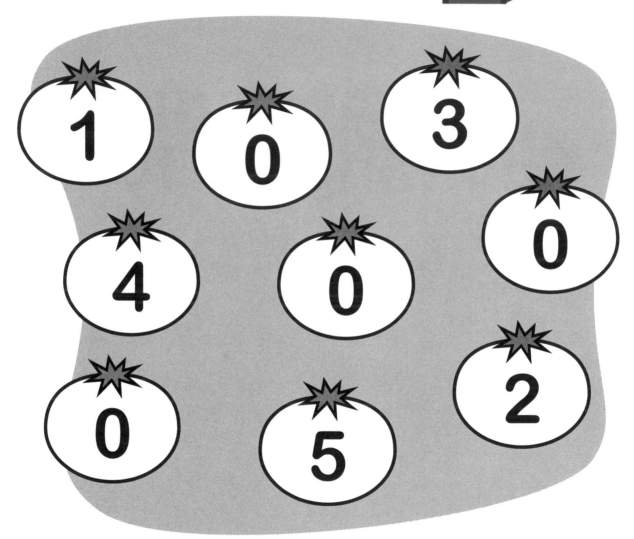

Can you circle the plate that has **0** meatballs?

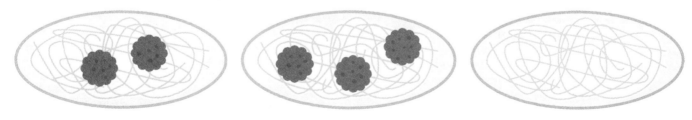

Rubber Ducks

It's bath time! Circle the bathtubs that have **1** rubber duck.

Which rubber ducks show the number **1**? Color them | yellow

2   1   3   0   1

Camping

Can you help the children find their tent?
Make a path to the tent by coloring all the trees with a number **2** green

2	2	2	5	6
3	4	2	2	2
5	1	0	4	2
1	4	1	3	2

Can you draw **2** smiley faces peeking out of the tent?

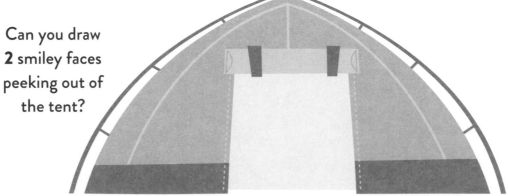

Bicycles

Can you count how many people are riding on each bicycle?
Draw a line to match each bicycle to the number you counted.

| 0 zero | 1 one | 2 two |

Pigs in Mud

What a lot of mud! Can you circle the pigs that have **3** mud splashes?

Which pig shows the number **3**? Color it **pink**

Birds

There are lots of birds singing in this tree.
Can you color the birds that have the number **4** blue ?

Can you circle **4** feathers?

Kittens

Look at the baskets of kittens. Circle all the baskets that have **5** kittens.

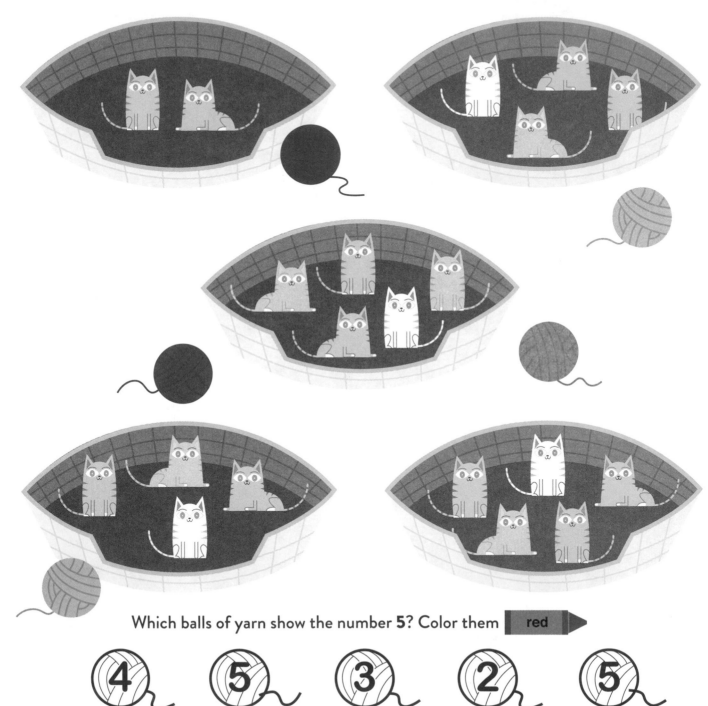

Which balls of yarn show the number **5**? Color them | red |

Ladybug Spots

Count the spots on the ladybugs.
Then draw a line to match each ladybug to the correct leaf.

Dog Bones

These dogs are hungry! Count how many bones each dog has in its bowl.
Then color the correct number.

Candy

There are lots of different candies in the picture, but they need some color!
Can you help color them? Count the dots in each shape and
use the code to find out what color each shape should be.

1 = red   2 = orange   3 = green   4 = purple   5 = yellow

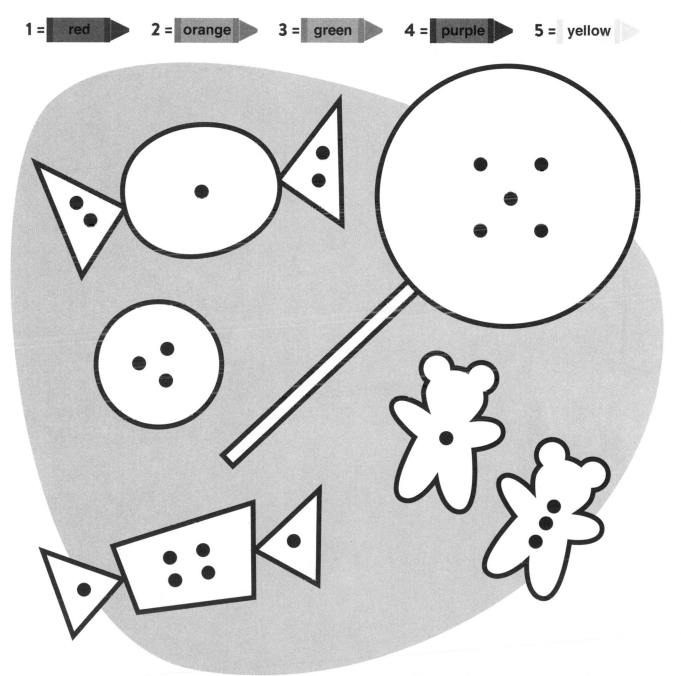

How Many Dots?

Can you count the dots on each die? Draw a line to the matching circle and trace the number inside.

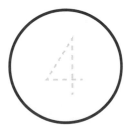

In the Meadow

There are lots of flowers in the meadow.
Color the flowers that show the number **6** orange ▶

Can you draw **6** petals
on this flower?

On the Pond

Look at this busy pond! Can you circle **7** frogs?

Color the frog that is sitting on the number **7** green

Slices

Can you count the toppings on each pizza slice?
Draw a line from each slice
to the number you counted.

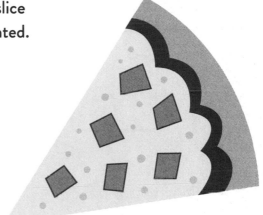

6
six

7
seven

Mouse House

Can you help the mouse find its house? Make a path to the house by coloring all the pieces of cheese with a number **8** yellow ▶

Can you draw
8 holes in the
mouse's cheese?

Balloon Bunches

Look at the colorful balloons. Circle the bunch that has **9** balloons.

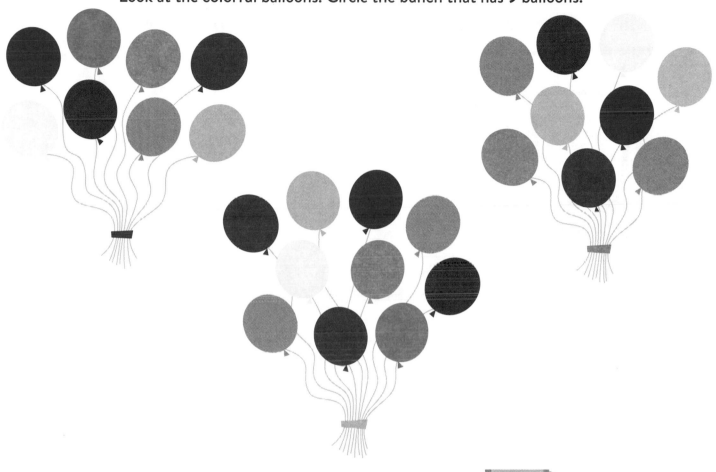

Can you color the balloons that show the number **9** `blue` ?

9 7 10 9 6

Basketballs

Look at the bouncing basketballs. Can you find the balls that show the number **10**? Draw a line to connect them to the net.

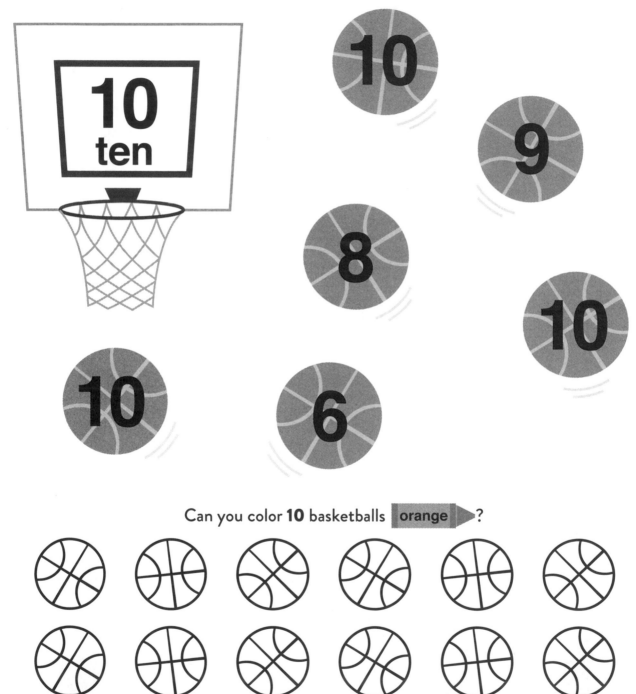

Can you color **10** basketballs orange ?

On the Bus

Can you count how many people are in each bus?
Draw a line to match each bus to the number you counted.

<table>
<tr><td>8
eight</td><td>9
nine</td><td>10
ten</td></tr>
</table>

Buzz Buzz

Who has landed on the flower? Use the code to color the picture.

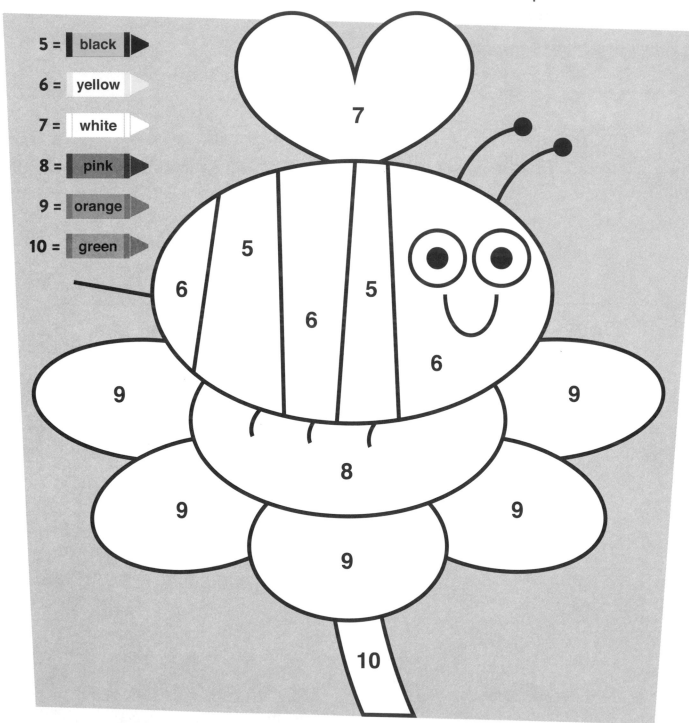

5 = black
6 = yellow
7 = white
8 = pink
9 = orange
10 = green

Weather

Can you count the weather pictures in each group?
Draw a line from each group to the matching circle and trace the number inside.

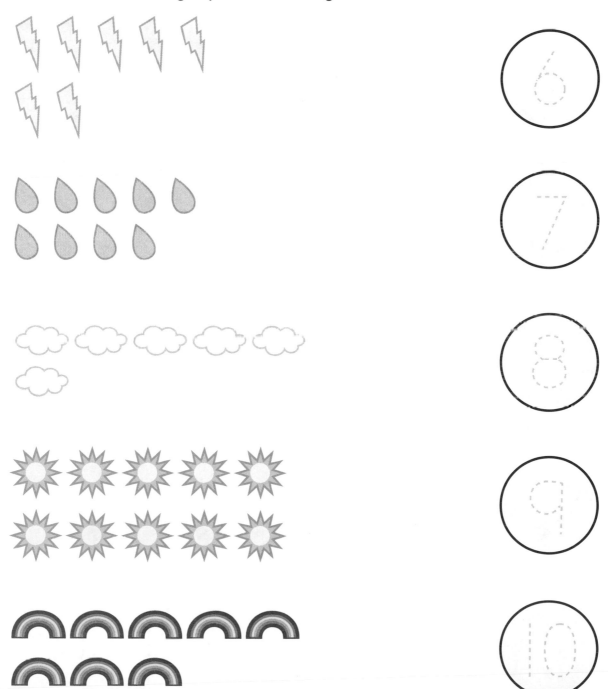

Going Home

Can you help the alien get back to its planet?
Follow the numbers in order from **1** to **10** to find the way.

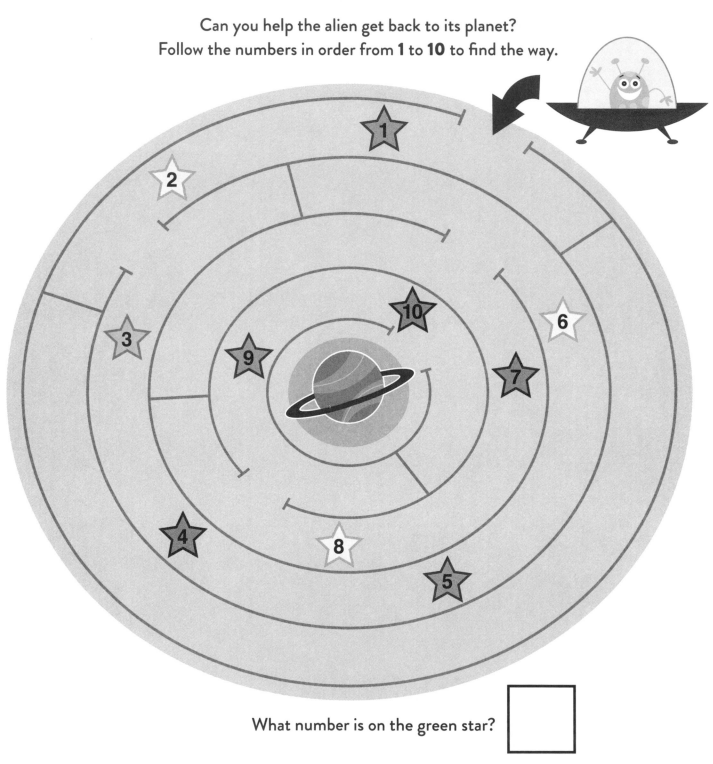

What number is on the green star?

Schools

Look at each school and count the happy faces inside. Trace the number you counted.

Put a checkmark (✓) next to the school that has a red door.

Firefighting

Can you help finish the picture of the fire truck?
Connect the dots in order by starting at **1** and counting all the way to **10**.

Then color the fire truck   red ▶

Can you fill in the missing numbers
on the firefighter's hose?

Hats

Look at all the children. Can you find and circle the **6** children who are wearing hats?

How many **blue** hats are there?	How many **red** hats are there?	How many hats have **stripes**?

Off to the Ball

Cinderella is getting ready to go to the ball. Can you connect the dots to finish her carriage? Start at the ⭐ and count backward from 10 to 1.

Then color the carriage.

Stargazing

These children are looking at the night sky.
Can you draw lines to match each star picture to the correct child?

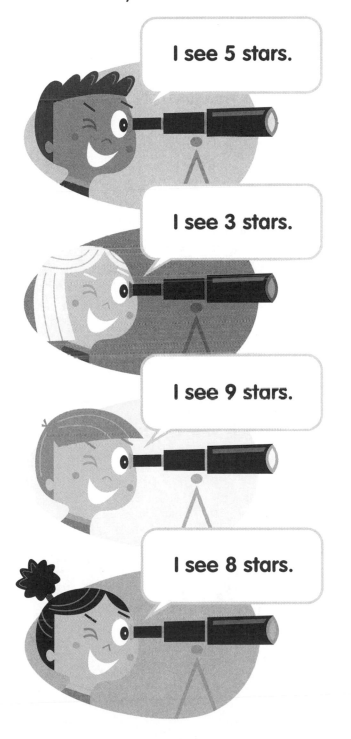

Soccer Shirts

Look at each group of soccer shirts. What number comes next?
Write the missing number in the box.

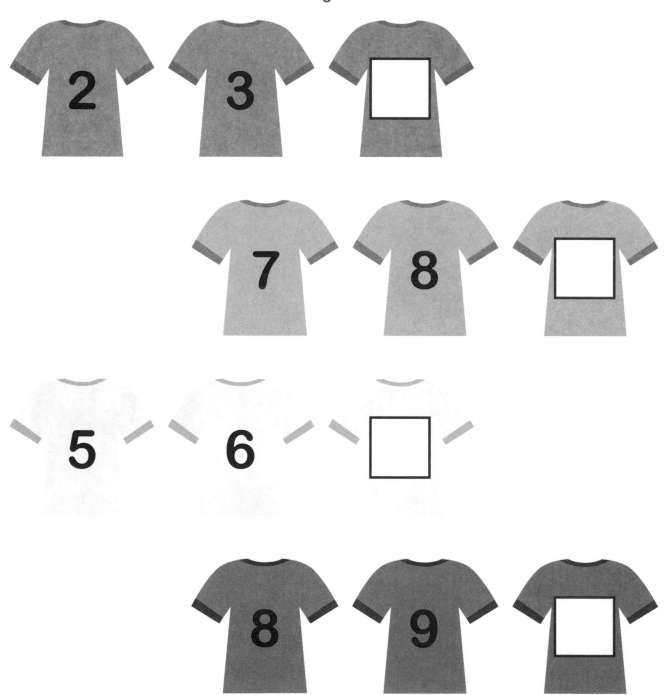

Looking for Land

This boat is lost! Can you help it get to the island?
Start at **10** and follow the numbers in order as you count backward to **1**.

Popcorn

What a lot of popcorn! For each row, look at the numbers on the popcorn boxes. Can you draw a line to the number that comes next?

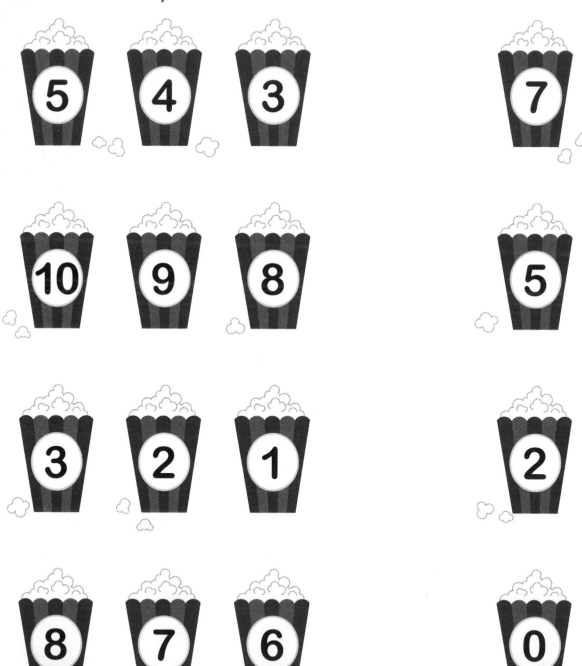

Chapter 2

Comparing Numbers

Once children learn to identify numbers and what they mean, they're ready to start comparing them. The puzzles in this chapter feature numbers up to 10 *in relation to each other*. Your child will begin by comparing objects in groups, like candles on cakes or dots on mugs. Later puzzles compare two written numerals. While doing these puzzles, your child will become familiar with language used to make comparisons, such as *more*, *less*, and *the same*.

Candles

Look at all the birthday cakes! Can you draw a line to connect the cakes that have the **same** number of candles?

Doughnuts

These doughnuts look tasty! For each pair of plates,
circle the one that has **more** doughnuts.

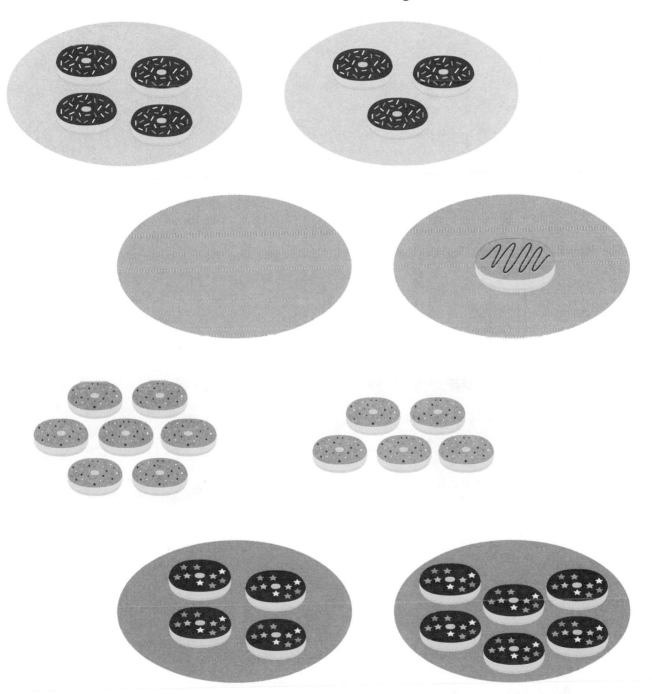

Collecting Shells

These two children have been enjoying collecting shells on the beach.

Who has **more** shells?
Check the correct box.

Mugs

Here are some dotty mugs. Can you count the dots on each one?
Color the two mugs that have the **same** number of dots.

Pets

I have **2** pets.

Can you put a checkmark (✓) next to the children who have **more** pets than me?

Draw a smiley face 🙂 next to your favorite pet.

Dinosaur Eggs

In each row, there are two groups of dinosaur eggs.
Can you circle the group that has **fewer** eggs?

 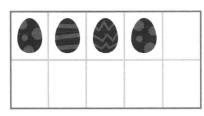 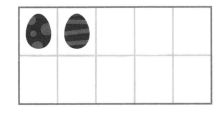

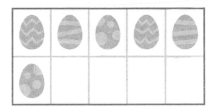  

 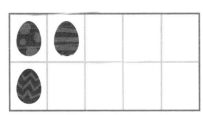 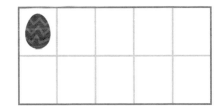

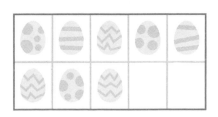 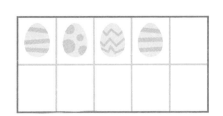 

Treasure Chests

These pirates have found some buried treasure!
Can you count the coins in each chest?

Draw a happy face
on the pirate
who has **more**.

Draw a sad face
on the pirate
who has **less**.

Color all the coins
yellow ▶

Cherries

Mmm—yummy cherries! For each pair of cherries, color the **bigger** number red

7   4

3   5

8   6

0   2

10   1

Ice Cream Cones

Count the scoops of ice cream on the cone. Can you draw scoops
of ice cream on the empty cone so that both cones have the **same** number?

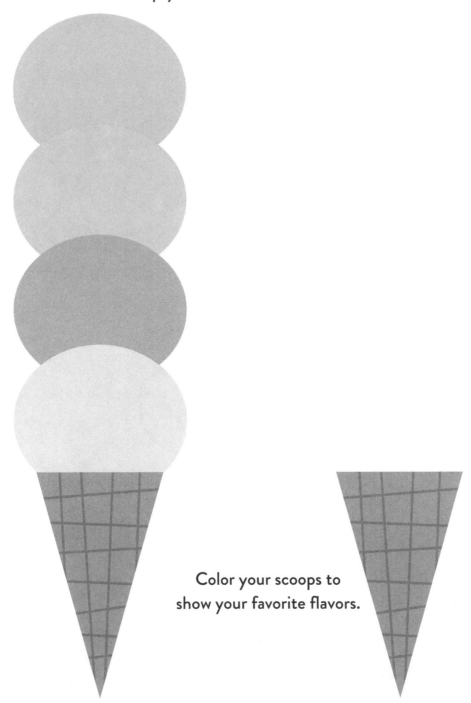

Color your scoops to
show your favorite flavors.

Umbrellas

These colorful umbrellas will keep the rain off.
For each pair of umbrellas, can you circle the **smaller** number?

Fall Leaves

These two children have been making piles with the fallen leaves.
Can you count how many leaves are in each pile? Write the number in the box.

leaves

leaves

Who has **more** leaves? Color their shirt blue

Who has **less** leaves? Color their shirt red

Chapter 3

Introducing Adding and Subtracting

This chapter offers a very gentle introduction to the concepts of _addition_ and _subtraction_. For children at this age, addition can be introduced as the idea of _putting numbers together_, and subtraction as _taking away_. These puzzles are simple and only involve addition and subtraction within 5. All of these puzzles have pictures to help your child visualize the equation. Encourage your child to use the pictures to help them as they do each puzzle. It can help to have physical objects like blocks or small toys nearby to demonstrate putting together and taking away.

Jellyfish

There are **2** jellyfish swimming near the seaweed.

Along come **2** more jellyfish.

How many jellyfish are there altogether? Find the answer and trace the number.

    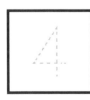

Insects

Here are lots of different insects. Use the pictures to help you finish each number sentence. Then draw a line from each picture to the flower with the correct answer.

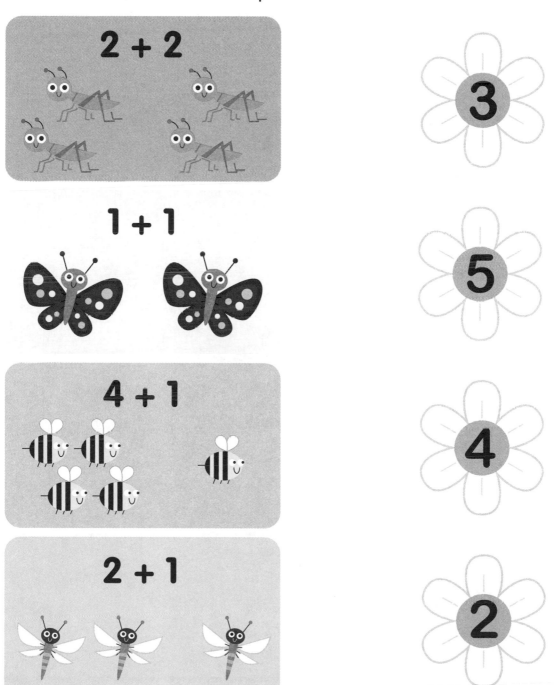

2 + 2

1 + 1

4 + 1

2 + 1

3

5

4

2

Piggy Banks

I have **3** coins in my piggy bank.

My sister has **2** coins in her piggy bank.

How many coins do we have altogether?

Draw the coins in the box.

Alligators

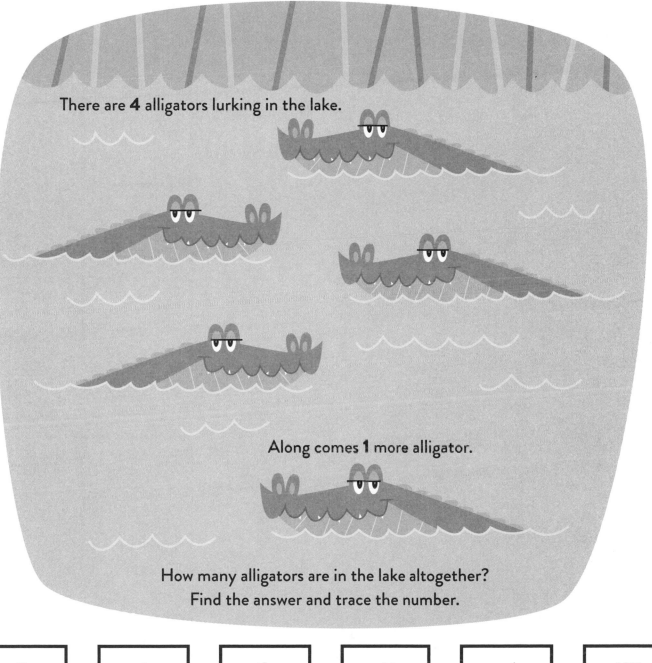

There are **4** alligators lurking in the lake.

Along comes **1** more alligator.

How many alligators are in the lake altogether?
Find the answer and trace the number.

Oranges and Lemons

Here are some oranges and lemons. Use the fruit pictures in each row to help you finish the number sentence. Write your answer in the box.

$$3 + 0 = \boxed{}$$

$$1 + 2 = \boxed{}$$

$$2 + 3 = \boxed{}$$

$$1 + 3 = \boxed{}$$

Dragons

There are **3** dragons flying around the castle.

A knight arrives and scares away **1** dragon.

How many dragons are left? Find the answer and trace the number.

| 0 | 1 | 2 | 3 | 4 | 5 |

Hearts

Use the heart pictures to help you finish each number sentence.
Draw a line to the heart with the correct answer.

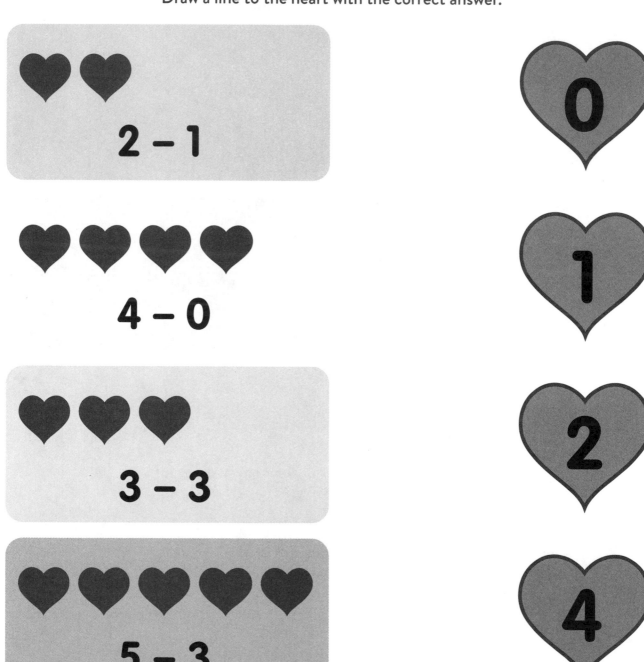

2 – 1

4 – 0

3 – 3

5 – 3

0

1

2

4

Pancakes

There are **4** pancakes in the pan.

My brother takes **2** pancakes for his breakfast.

How many pancakes are left in the pan?

Draw the pancakes in the box.

Apple Tree

There are **5** red apples on the tree.

A girl picks **5** apples to make an apple pie.

How many apples are left on the tree? Find the answer and trace the number.

Farm Animals

Look at each group of farm animals. Use the pictures to help you finish each number sentence. Write your answer in the box.

$$5 - 1 =$$

$$2 - 0 =$$

$$4 - 3 =$$

$$1 - 1 =$$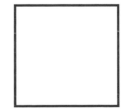

Chapter 4

Sizes and Measurements

At this age, your child may not be ready to grasp the concept of measuring using tools like rulers, scales, or measuring cups. But you can start with the very basics, like matching objects according to size, or comparing different-sized objects and deciding which is bigger or smaller. These puzzles help your child practice comparing measurable attributes like height, width, and weight. When making comparisons, your child may be asked to compare just two things or to pick the smallest/tallest/shortest from a group of objects. Some puzzles show nonstandard units of measurement—for example, measuring toys using a tower of blocks. While measuring, your child will enjoy meeting the three bears, as well as taking a trip to the big city.

The Three Bears

Here are three bears and their bowls of porridge.
Draw a line to match each bear to the correct bowl.

My bowl
is small.

My bowl
is medium-
sized.

My bowl
is big.

Put a checkmark (✓) next to the bear wearing **blue**.

Plants

Look at each pair of plants.
Color the pot of the plant that is **taller**.

Put a checkmark (✓) next to the plant that has **4** flowers.

Animal Faces

Look at each pair of animal faces.
Which face is **wider**? Put a checkmark (✓) next to it.

Can you circle the animal on the
page that has the **longest** ears?

Toys

Can you count how many blocks **tall** each toy is?
Find and trace the correct number.

Which Weighs More?

Think about these objects in real life.
For each pair, choose the one you think is **heavier**. Then color the box.

mouse	truck

apple	house

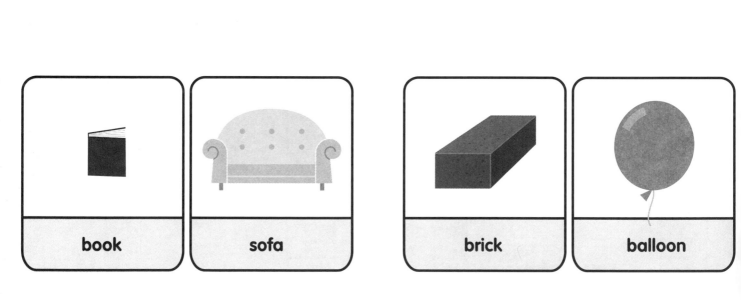

book	sofa

brick	balloon

Will It Fit?

Do you think each object will fit in its box?
Color the 🙂 for yes. Color the 🙁 for no.

  or

   or

  or

   or

Giraffes

Look at each pair of giraffes. Can you circle the giraffe that is **shorter**?

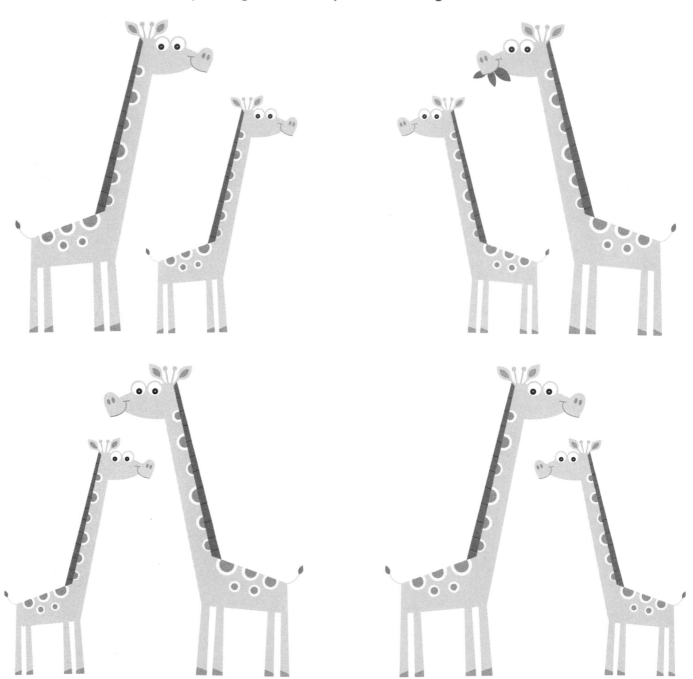

Which giraffe is eating leaves? Put a checkmark (✓) next to it.

Wiggly Worms

Here are three pairs of wiggly worms. In each pair, one worm is long and one is short. Can you draw a hat on the worm that is **long**?

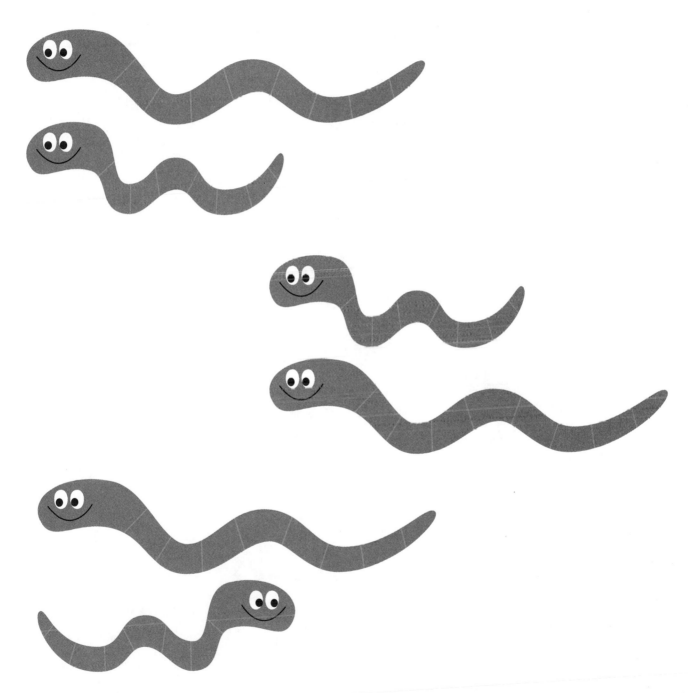

Rainforest Friends

Here are some creatures that live in the rainforest.
For each row of creatures, can you circle the one that is the **biggest**?

Downtown

Look at all the buildings downtown. They are all different heights.

Color the **tallest** building red   Color the **shortest** building blue

Can you draw **2** clouds and **1** sun above the buildings?

Robots

Look closely at the robots in each group.
One robot is **smaller** than the rest. Can you circle it?

How many robots on this page have **orange** feet?

Chapter 5

Shapes and Patterns

Young children enjoy spotting shapes and patterns in everyday objects. These puzzles help your child to learn to identify and name basic shapes such as circles, triangles, rectangles, and squares. Your child will trace shapes, sort them, and spot them in different settings. Some puzzles focus on the properties of shapes—for example, how many sides or corners a shape has. Others feature simple repeating patterns made of objects, shapes, and colors.

Penguin Pals

Can you help the penguin get to his friends?
Find a path through the ice by coloring all the **squares**.

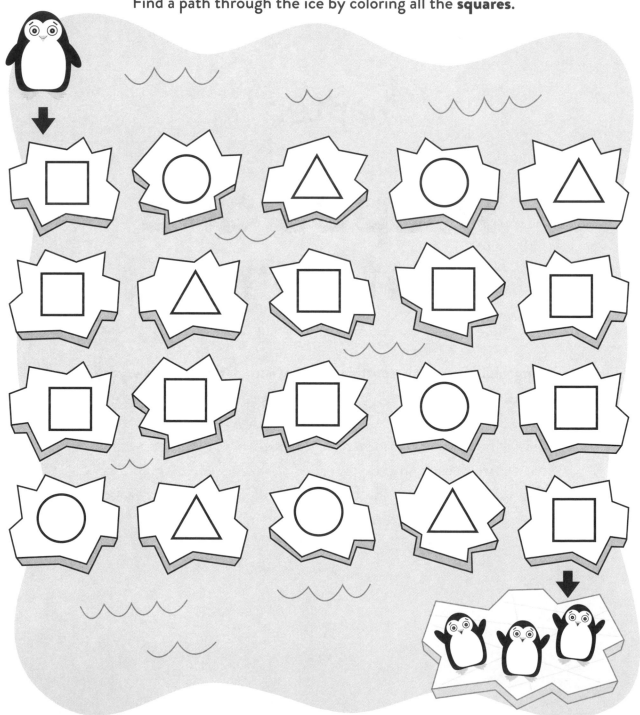

Clocks

Here are lots of different-shaped clocks.
Can you put a checkmark (✓) next to the clocks that are **circles**?

Circle or Square?

Some of these objects are **circles** and some are **squares**. Can you sort them?
Draw a line to connect each object to the correct shape.

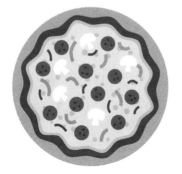
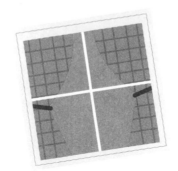

square

circle

Paint Splashes

Look at all the paint splashes! In each row, the colors make a pattern.

Can you color the last splash in each row to continue the pattern?

Find the Triangles

This picture is full of **triangles.** Can you find them all?
Draw a circle around each triangle you spot.

How many **triangles** did you find?

Home Sweet Home

Can you help finish the picture of a house?
Trace the **rectangles** and then color the picture.

Beads

Look at each string of beads. The shapes make a pattern.
Which shape should come next? Trace the line to the correct bead.

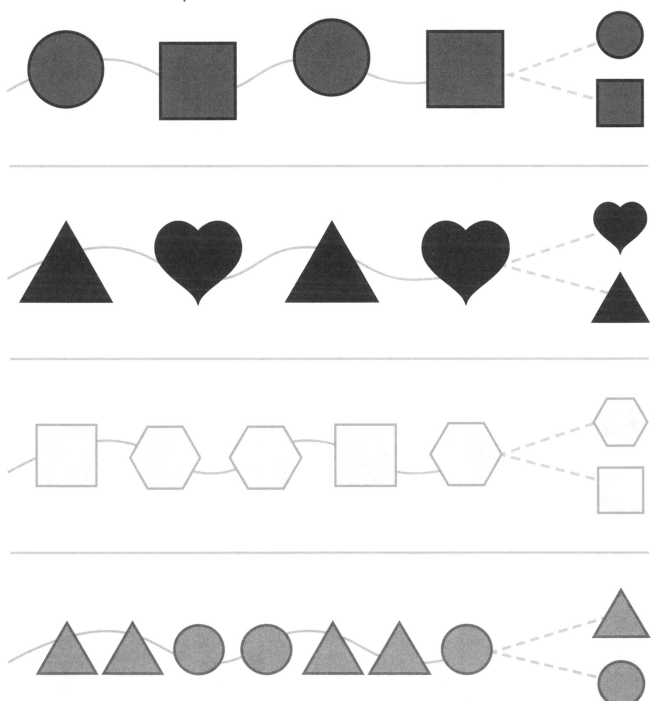

Triangle or Rectangle?

Some of these objects are **triangles** and some are **rectangles**. Can you sort them?
Draw a line to connect each object to the correct shape.

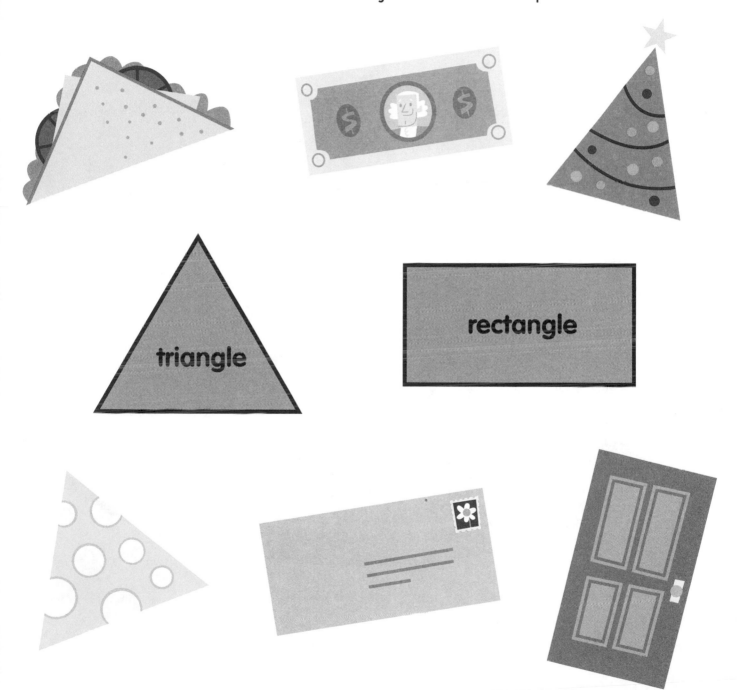

Crown

Look at this crown, fit for a king or queen.
There are **circles**, **diamonds**, and **triangles** on the crown. Can you trace them?

Next, color the shapes.

Color the ◇ green   Color the ○ red   Color the △ blue

Beach Patterns

Look at the patterns made from things you might find at the beach.
For each pattern, color the box to show what comes next.

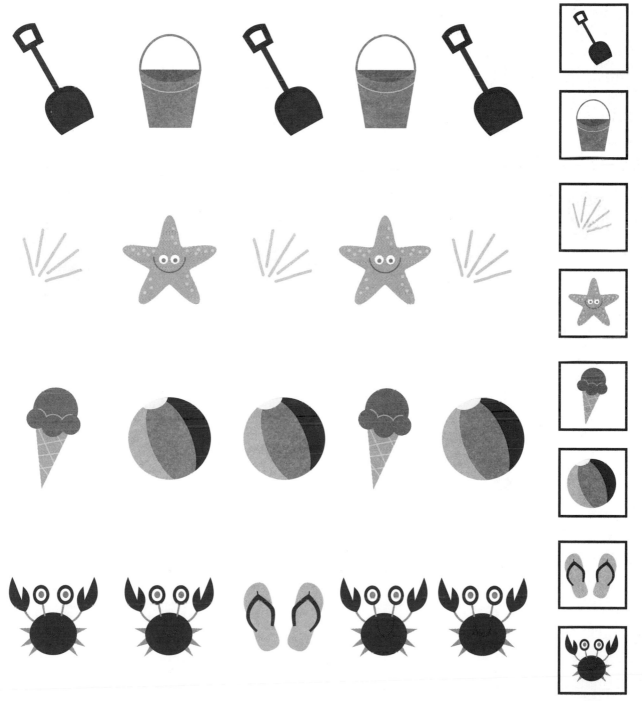

Shape Maze

Follow the path through the maze. It will lead you to a shape!

START
HERE

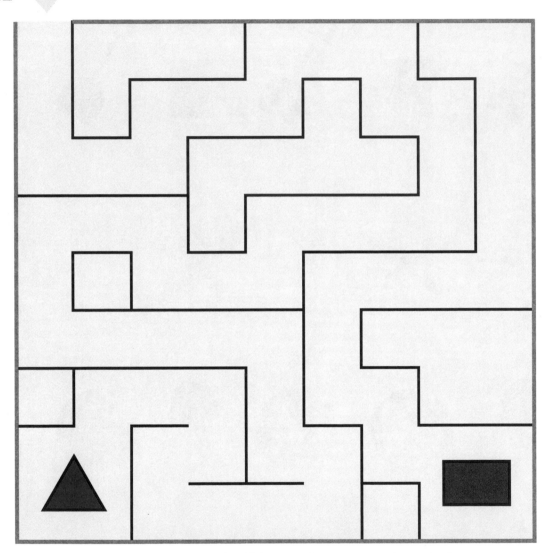

Which shape did you find? Trace the correct shape below.

 **or**

Birthday

Someone is having a birthday today!
Look closely at the picture. Circle all the **ovals** you find.

HAPPY BIRTHDAY

Can you draw an **oval** balloon above the cake?

Odd One Out

Can you circle the shape in each row that doesn't belong?

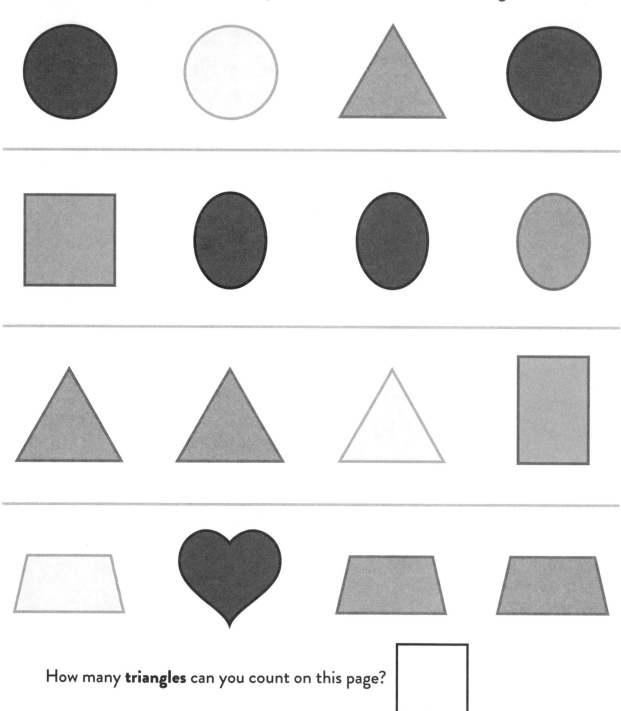

How many **triangles** can you count on this page?

Scarecrow

Can you color the scarecrow's clothes? Look at the shape on each piece of clothing, and then use the code to color the outfit.

△ yellow
▭ brown
◯ red
♡ blue

Luggage

Here are three pieces of luggage. Each one is a different shape.
Can you draw a line to match each person to their luggage?

Shape Faces

Can you count how many sides each shape has?
Color all the shapes with **4** sides.

Hats and Mittens

Let's create some color patterns with these hats and mittens.

First, choose two colors: one for the hats and one for the mittens.
Then color the crayons.

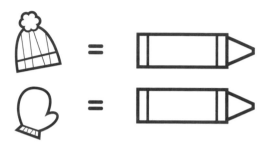

Now color the pictures to make these two patterns.

Pattern 1

Pattern 2

Chapter 6

Position Words

Position puzzles let your child practice using words like *inside*, *up*, *down*, *behind*, and *between*. Your child will be asked to provide answers in lots of different ways. Some puzzles will require them to circle or put a checkmark next to a picture or object, while others will ask them to color the position word being shown.

White Rabbits

Look at all the white rabbits and hats.
Can you circle all the rabbits that are **inside** the hats?

Mountain Goats

Look at each picture. Is the goat **up** or **down** the mountain?
Color the correct word.

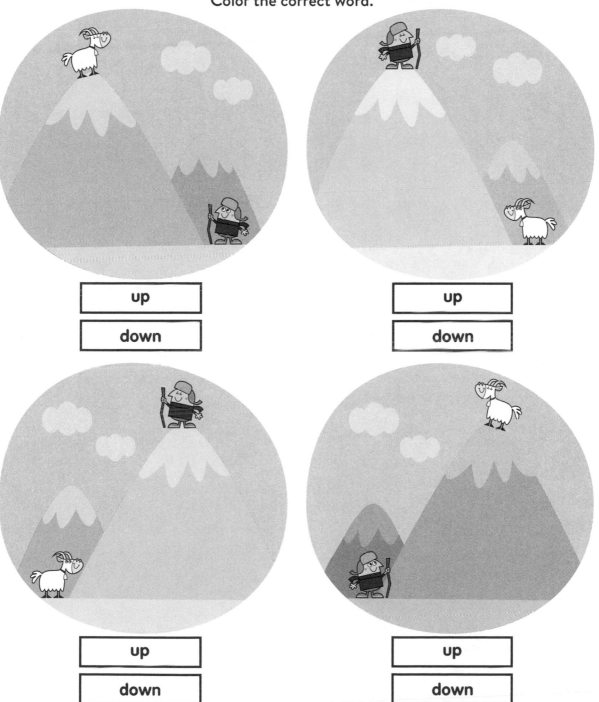

up
down

up
down

up
down

up
down

Planets

In each picture, there are two planets.
Can you put a checkmark (✓) next to the planet that is **nearer** to the rocket?

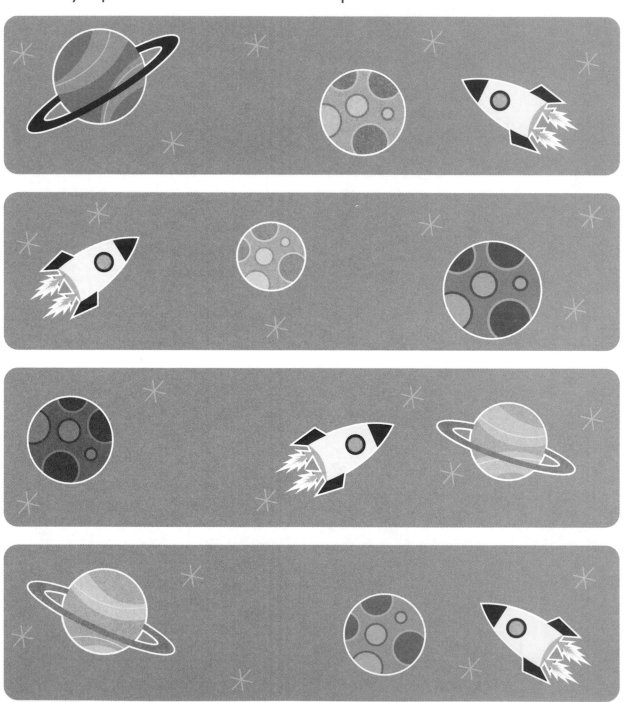

Superheroes

Here are two superheroes, off to save the day!
Look at where each superhero is in the sky.

Which superhero is **high** in the sky?
Color their cape green

Which superhero is **low** in the sky?
Color their cape yellow

Clouds

For each picture, can you say if the circled object
is **above** or **below** the clouds? Color the correct word.

above

below

above

below

above

below

above

below

Seaweed

Look at these pictures of fish.
Can you circle the pictures where the fish is **between** the seaweeds?

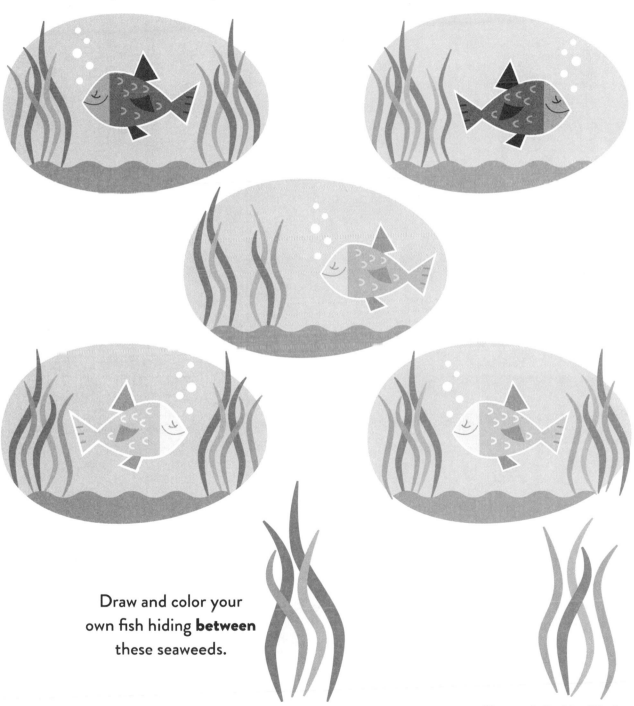

Draw and color your
own fish hiding **between**
these seaweeds.

Inside or Outside?

Look at the different objects. Do you think they belong **inside** the house or **outside** the house? Draw a line to match each object to where it belongs.

inside

outside

Peanut Butter and Jelly

Look at the food on each shelf. Is the peanut butter **beside** the jelly?
If yes, color the 🙂. If no, color the 🙁.

Elephant and Friends

Look at the elephant and its friend in each picture.
Is the elephant on the **right** or the **left**? Color the correct word.

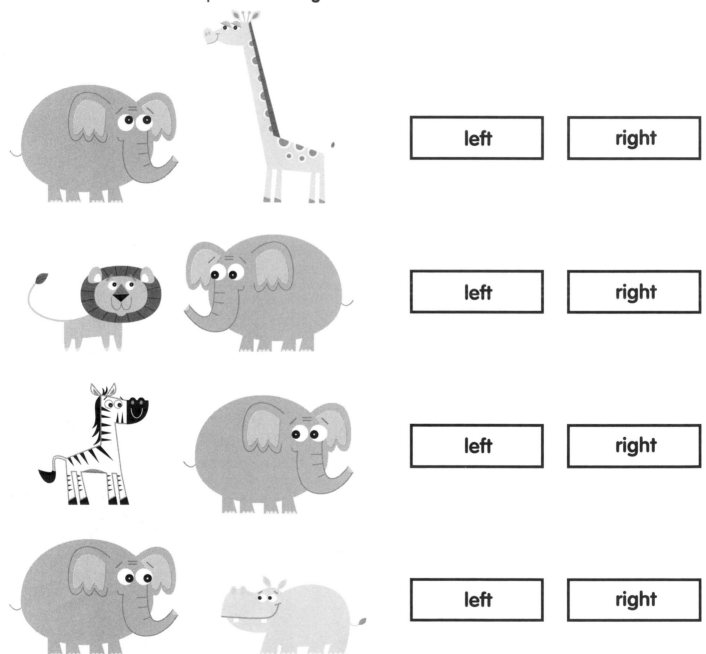

| left | right |

| left | right |

| left | right |

| left | right |

Draw a smiley face 🙂 next to your favorite animal.

In the Ocean

Can you spot the two seahorses in the picture?
Put a checkmark (✓) next to the seahorse that is **near** the mermaid.
Circle the seahorse that is **far** from the mermaid.

Can you draw a fish **near** the octopus?

Hide and Seek

There are lots of children playing hide and seek. Circle all the children hiding **behind** the trees.

Which dog is **in front** of the bench?
Put a checkmark (✔) next to it.

Chapter 7

Matching and Sorting

At a very young age, children begin to learn the concepts of *same and different*, and to notice that some objects can be matched up. These concepts help them to understand the idea of sorting. With these puzzles, your child will practice matching shapes, colors, and numbers. They will also sort objects according to their type, size, and color, as well as how many of a certain attribute something has (for example, how many humps on a camel). Preschoolers love to sort things because it helps them to make sense of their world.

Whose Mail?

Can you help sort the mail? Draw a line to match each letter to the house that is the **same** color.

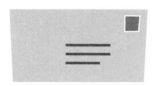

Books

Can you help sort the books into **different** sizes?

Color the big books orange

Color the small books purple

Camels

Count how many humps each camel has.

Circle the camels with **1** hump in blue   Circle the camels with **2** humps in green

Are there more camels with **1** hump or **2**? Check the correct box.

☐ 1 hump   ☐ 2 humps

Vegetables

Look at the two vegetables in each circle. Are they the **same** or **different**?
Draw a line to match each circle to the correct word.

same	different

 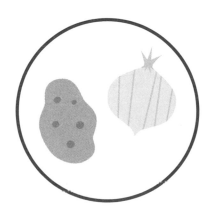 

Backpacks

Look at all the backpacks. Draw lines to connect the ones that match.

Color this backpack so that the two backpacks match.

Things That Go

Here are six different vehicles. Can you sort them into their **different** colors?
Draw a line from each vehicle to the correct paint splash.

yellow

green

blue

Sorting Laundry

The laundry is clean, but all jumbled up! Can you help sort it?

Color all the socks **red**

Color all the T-shirts **blue**

Color all the pants **green**

Doors

Look at the colored door in each row. What number do you see?
Find and color the door that has the matching number.

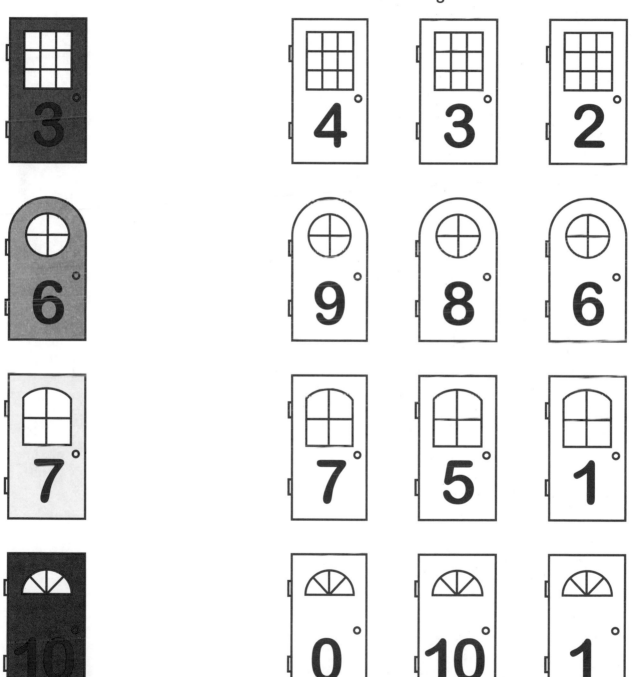

Picture Frames

This family has decorated the wall with pictures in frames.
Can you draw lines to connect the picture frames that are the **same** shape?

Draw a smiley face
on the person in the
big square frame.

Bears

These bears are sorted into **different** color groups, but there are some mistakes!
Circle the **4** bears that are in the wrong group.

Color the bears in this last group.

Coats

Look at the two coats: one with circles and one with squares. These coats need buttons! Can you draw a line to match each button to the correct coat?

Now, color the buttons.

Color the ⊙ red ▸   Color the ▢ yellow ▹

Answers

Chapter 1

Page 8 • Spaghetti and Meatballs

1 0 3
4 0 0
0 5 2

Page 9 • Rubber Ducks

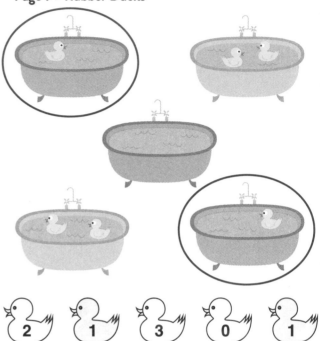

Page 10 • Camping

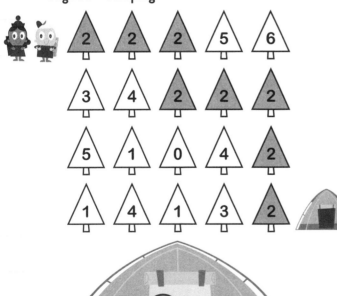

2	2	2	5	6
3	4	2	2	2
5	1	0	4	2
1	4	1	3	2

Page 11 • Bicycles

Page 12 • Pigs in Mud

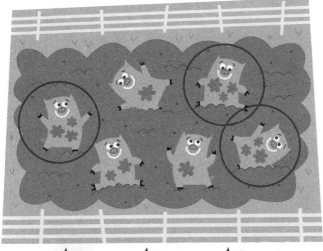

Page 13 • Birds

Circle any 4 feathers

Page 14 • Kittens

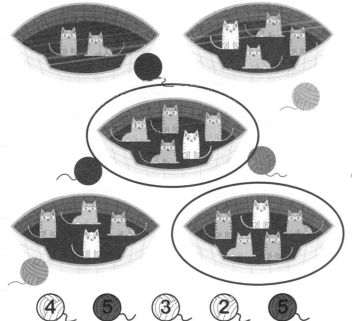

Page 15 • Ladybug Spots

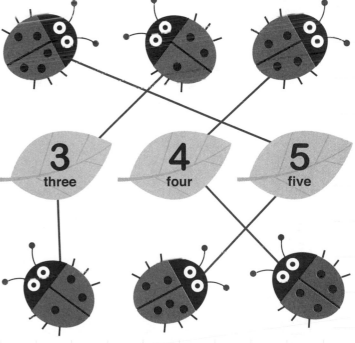

Page 16 • Dog Bones

Page 17 • Candy

Page 18 • How Many Dots?

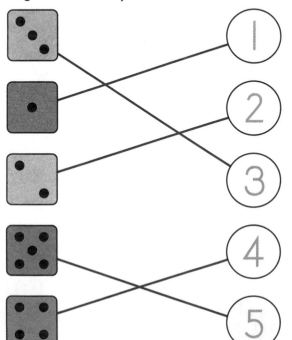

Page 19 • In the Meadow

Page 20 • On the Pond

Circle any 7 frogs

9 8 7

Page 21 • Slices

6
six

7
seven

Page 22 • Mouse House

9	7	10	8	8
10	6	8	8	6
8	8	8	9	7
8	7	6	10	9

HOME

Page 23 • Balloon Bunches

9 7 10 9 6

Page 24 • Basketballs

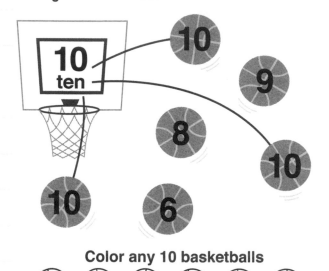

Color any 10 basketballs

Page 25 • On the Bus

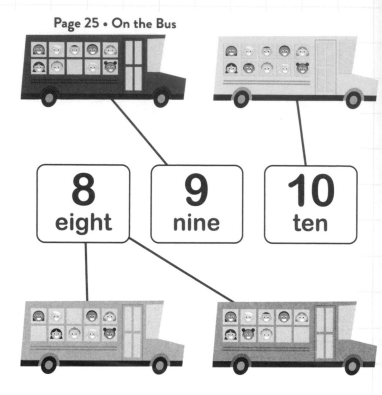

Page 26 • Buzz Buzz

Page 27 • Weather

Page 28 • Going Home

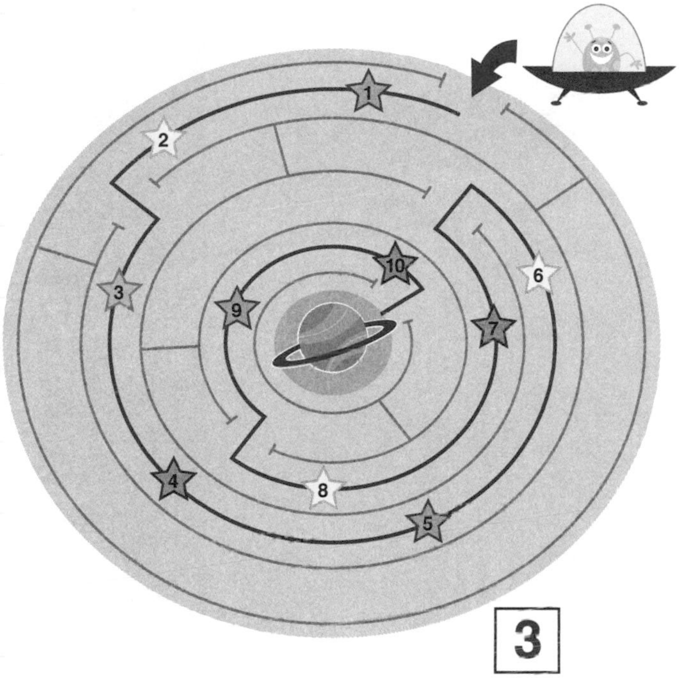

3

Page 29 • Schools

Page 30 • Firefighting

Page 31 • Hats

3   1   2

Page 32 • Off to the Ball

Page 33 • Stargazing

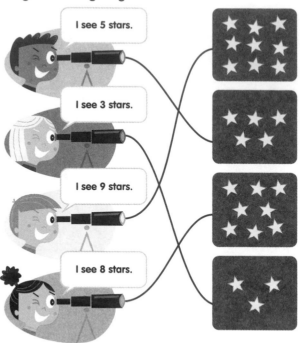

Page 34 • Soccer Shirts

Page 35 • Looking for Land

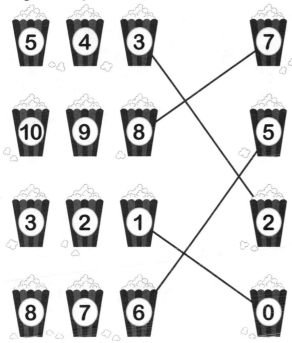

Chapter 2

Page 38 • Candles

Page 39 • Doughnuts

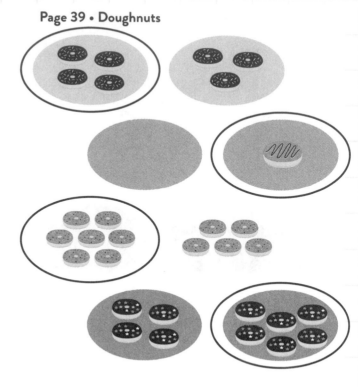

Page 40 • Collecting Shells

Page 41 • Mugs

Page 42 • Pets

Page 43 • Dinosaur Eggs

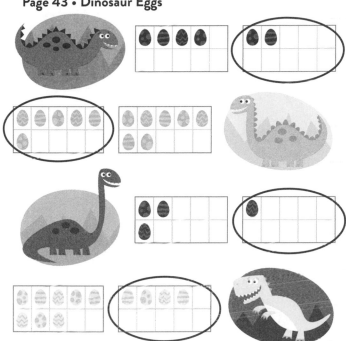

Page 44 • Treasure Chests

Page 45 • Cherries

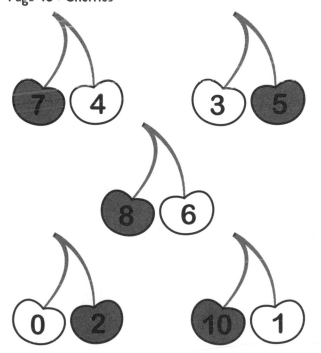

Page 46 • Ice Cream Cones

Page 47 • Umbrellas

5　②　①　3

J　J　J　J

8　⓪

J　J

⑥　9　　10　④

J　J

Page 48 • Fall Leaves

10 leaves

8 leaves

Chapter 3

Page 50 • Jellyfish

Page 51 • Insects

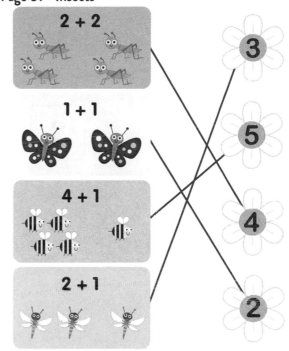

Page 52 • Piggy Banks

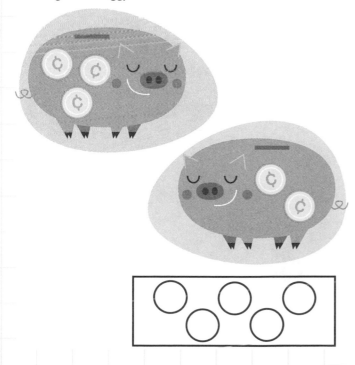

Page 53 • Alligators

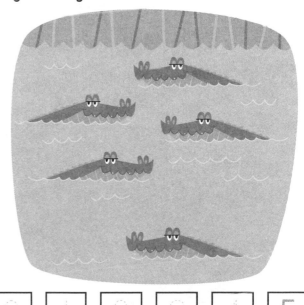

Page 54 • Oranges and Lemons

3 + 0 = **3**

1 + 2 = **3**

2 + 3 = **5**

1 + 3 = **4**

Page 55 • Dragons

Page 56 • Hearts

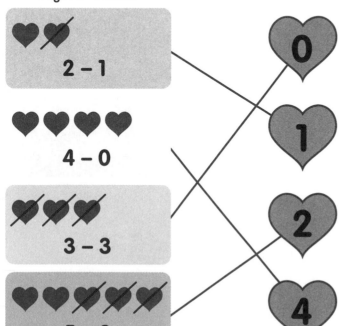

Page 57 • Pancakes

Page 58 • Apple Tree

| 0 | 1 | 2 | 3 | 4 | 5 |

Page 59 • Farm Animals

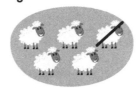

5 – 1 = **4**

2 – 0 = **2**

4 – 3 = **1**

1 – 1 = **0**

Chapter 4

Page 62 • The Three Bears

My bowl is small.

My bowl is medium-sized. ✓

My bowl is big.

Page 63 • Plants

Page 64 • Animal Faces

Page 65 • Toys

| 5 |
| 4 |
| 3 |
| 2 |
| 1 |

2 3 4

| 5 |
| 4 |
| 3 |
| 2 |
| 1 |

3 4 5

| 5 |
| 4 |
| 3 |
| 2 |
| 1 |

0 1 2

| 5 |
| 4 |
| 3 |
| 2 |
| 1 |

2 3 4

Page 66 • Which Weighs More?

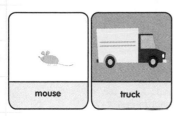

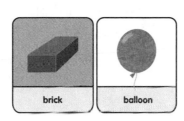

Page 67 • Will It Fit?

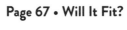

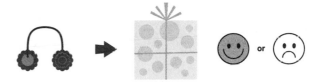

Page 68 • Giraffes

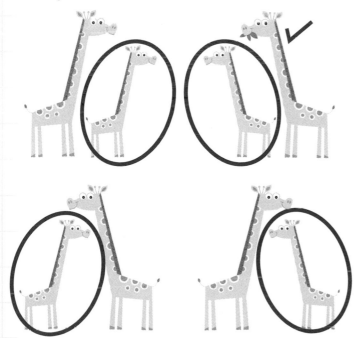

Page 69 • Wiggly Worms

Page 70 • Rainforest Friends

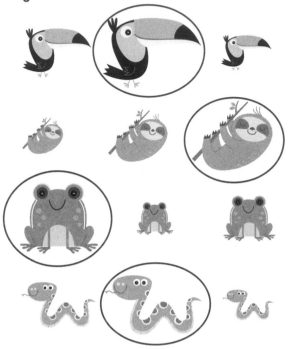

Page 71 • Downtown

Page 72 • Robots

2

Chapter 5

Page 74 • Penguin Pals

Page 75 • Clocks

Page 76 • Circle or Square?

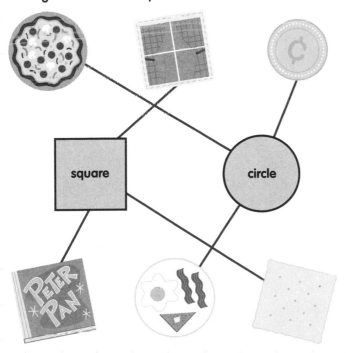

Page 77 • Paint Splashes

Can you color the last splash in each row to continue the pattern?

Page 78 • Find the Triangles

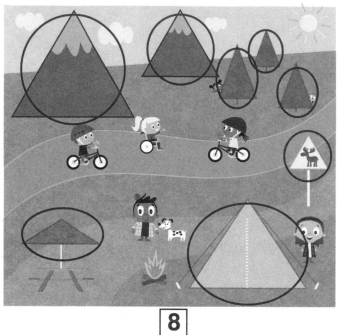

8

Page 79 • Home Sweet Home

Page 80 • Beads

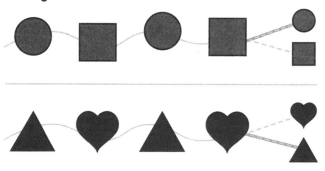

Page 81 • Triangle or Rectangle?

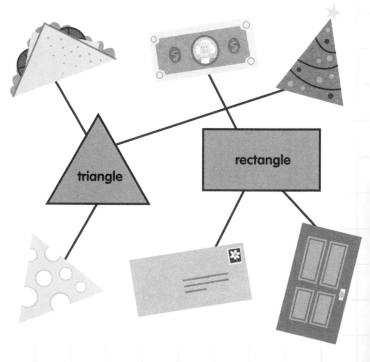

triangle

rectangle

Page 82 • Crown

Page 83 • Beach Patterns

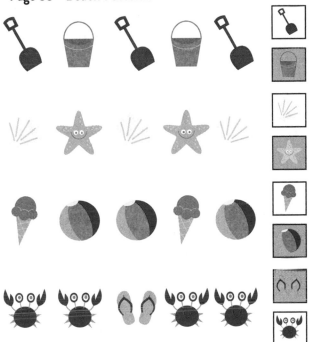

Page 84 • Shape Maze

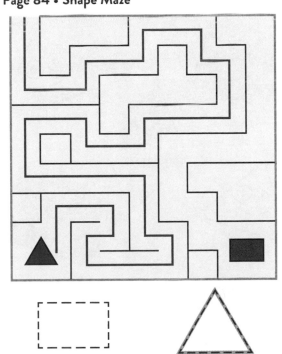

Page 85 • Birthday

Page 86 • Odd One Out

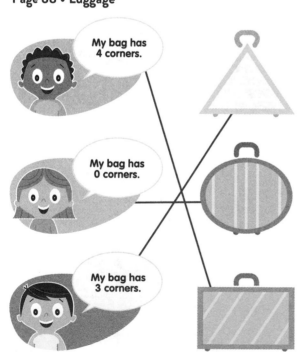

Page 87 • Scarecrow

Page 88 • Luggage

Page 89 • Shape Faces

Here is an example using red and green

Chapter 6

Page 92 • White Rabbits

Page 93 • Mountain Goats

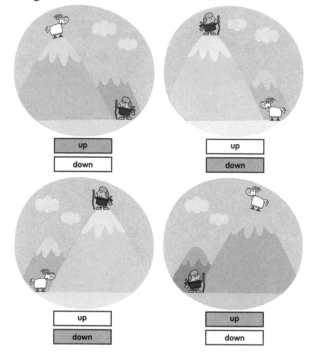

Page 94 • Planets

Page 95 • Superheroes

Page 96 • Clouds

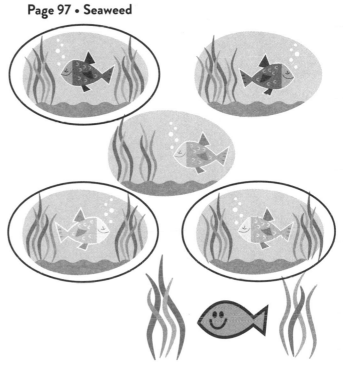

above / **below**

above / below

above / below

above / **below**

Page 97 • Seaweed

Page 98 • Inside or Outside?

inside

outside

Page 99 • Peanut Butter and Jelly

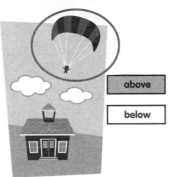

Jelly   Pineapple   mustard   Peanut Butter

Juice   Peanut Butter   Jelly   Ketchup

Peanut Butter   Corn   Jelly   Soup

Page 100 • Elephant and Friends

left | **right**

left | right

left | right

left | **right**

Page 101 • In the Ocean

Page 102 • Hide and Seek

Chapter 7

Page 104 • Whose Mail?

Page 105 • Books

Page 106 • Camels

Page 107 • Vegetables

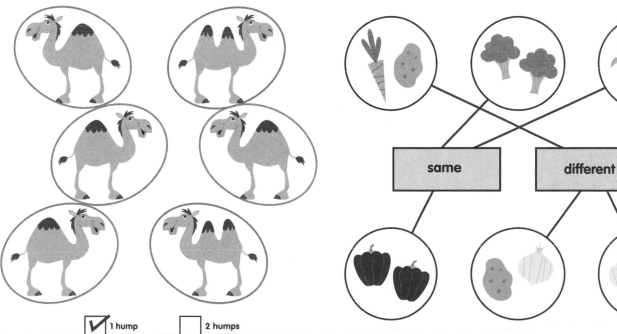

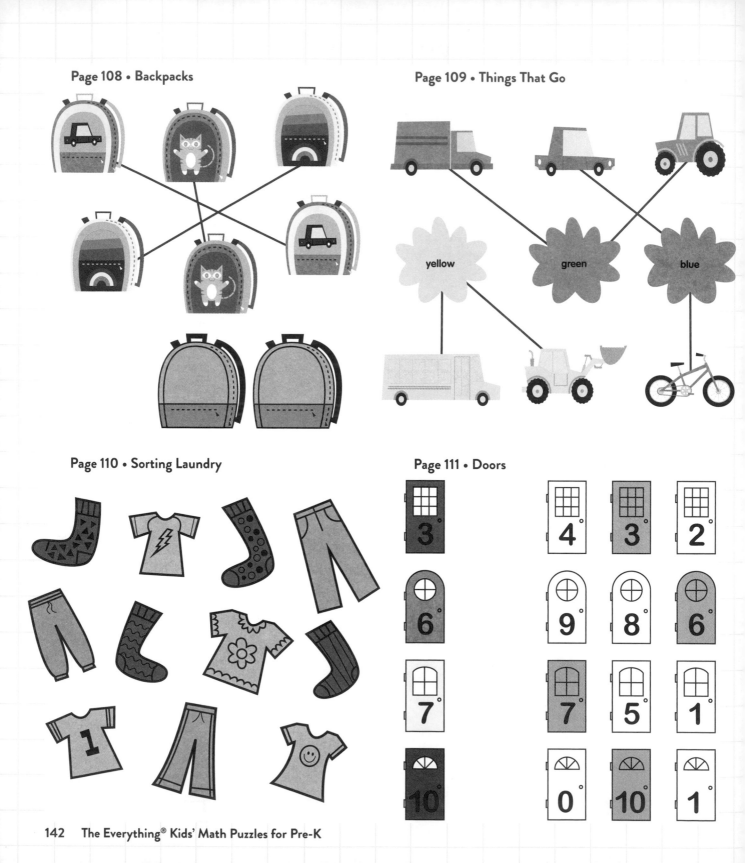

Page 108 • Backpacks

Page 109 • Things That Go

yellow   green   blue

Page 110 • Sorting Laundry

Page 111 • Doors

3 4 3 2

6 9 8 6

7 7 5 1

10 0 10 1

Page 112 • Picture Frames

Page 113 • Bears

Page 114 • Coats

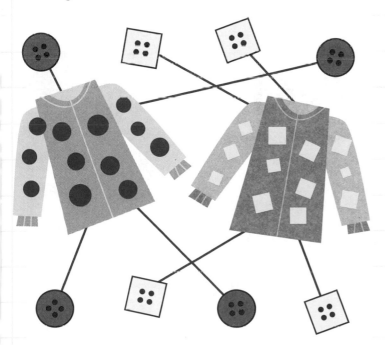

MATH PUZZLES AND ACTIVITIES your kindergarten student is sure to love!

"Everything you want in a kid's book"
— Associated Press

Curriculum-based activities made fun!

K

THE
EVERYTHING
KIDS'
Math Puzzles
for
Kindergarten

Learn about Counting, Measuring, Adding, and More with **100 Fun Puzzles!**

Hannah Whately

IMPROVE LEARNING FROM HOME!

PICK UP OR DOWNLOAD YOUR COPY TODAY!